THE AFRICAN AMERICAN
EXPERIENCE
FROM SLAVERY TO THE PRESIDENCY

THE GREAT MIGRATION
AND THE
HARLEM RENAISSANCE

EDITED BY
SABINA G. ARORA

Britannica®
Educational Publishing

IN ASSOCIATION WITH

ROSEN
EDUCATIONAL SERVICES

Published in 2016 by Britannica Educational Publishing (a trademark of Encyclopædia Britannica, Inc.) in association with The Rosen Publishing Group, Inc.
29 East 21st Street, New York, NY 10010

Distributed exclusively by Rosen Publishing.
To see additional Britannica Educational Publishing titles, go to rosenpublishing.com.

First Edition

Britannica Educational Publishing
J. E. Luebering: Director, Core Reference Group
Anthony L. Green: Editor, Compton's by Britannica

Rosen Publishing
Hope Lourie Killcoyne: Executive Editor
Sabina G. Arora: Editor
Nelson Sá: Art Director
Nicole Russo: Designer
Cindy Reiman: Photography Manager

Libary of Congress Cataloging-in-Publication Data

The great migration and the Harlem Renaissance/edited by Sabina G. Arora.—First edition.
        pages cm.—(The African American experience: From slavery to the presidency)
Includes bibliographical references and index.
ISBN 978-1-68048-045-0 (library bound)
1. Harlem Renaissance—Juvenile literature. 2. African Americans—History—1877–1964—Juvenile literature. 3. African American arts—20th century—Juvenile literature. 4. Harlem (New York, N.Y.)—Intellectual life—20th century—Juvenile literature. 5. New York (N.Y.)—Intellectual life—20th century—Juvenile literature. 6. African Americans—New York (State)—New York—Biography—Juvenile literature. I. Arora, Sabina G.
E185.6.G785 2016
305.896'0730747—dc23

2014039600

Manufactured in the United States of America

On the cover: (Left) A band performs at the Beaux Arts Ball of the National Urban League in the Savoy Ballroom, Harlem, 1949. The Savoy was a popular music hall during the Harlem Renaissance. (Right) The remarkable Harlem Renaissance performer and comedienne, Florence Mills.

Photo credits: Cover (Florence Mills portrait) John D. Kisch/Separate Cinema Archive/Archive Photos/Getty Images; cover (musicians) Gjon Mili/Time & Life Pictures/The Life Picture Collection/Getty Images; p. 5 New York Daily News/Getty Images; pp. 9, 12–13, 33, 41 Library of Congress, Washington, D.C.; p. 14 Charles Alburtus/Yale University; pp. 16–17 Encyclopædia Britannica, Inc.; p. 19 Jun Fujita/Chicago History Museum/Archive Photos/Getty Images; p. 22 Library of Congress, Washington, D.C., (LC-USZ61-1854); pp. 26–27 George Karger/Pix Inc./Time & Life Pictures/Getty Images; p. 28 Courtesy of Howard University, Washington, D.C.; p. 30 Stock Montage/Archive Photos/Getty Images; pp. 34–35, 66 © AP Images; p. 37 Robert W. Kelley/The Life Picture Collection/Getty Images; p. 39 Between the Covers Rare Books, Merchantville, NJ; pp. 42–43 Anthony Barboza/Archive Photos/Getty Images; pp. 46–47 Schomburg Center, NYPL/Art Resource, NY; p. 48 Image copyright © The Metropolitan Museum of Art, Image source: Art Resource, NY; p. 50 Future Expectations, photograph by James VanDerZee, c. 1925. Copyright © 2008 by Dover Publications, Inc. Electronic image © 2008 Dover Publications, Inc. All rights reserved; pp. 52–53 The New York Public Library/Art Resource, NY; p. 54 General Photographic Agency/Hulton Archive/Getty Images; p. 57 Library of Congress, Washington, D.C., Arthur Rothstein (neg. no. LC-USF34-005788-D); pp. 60–61 Robert Abbott Sengstacke/Archive Photos/Getty Images; p. 63 Thomas D. McAvoy/The Life Picture Collection/Getty Images; p. 65 Hulton Archive/Getty Images; interior pages background texture © iStockphoto.com/ Piotr Krzeslak.

CONTENTS

INTRODUCTION

When slavery was abolished in 1865, blacks were an over-whelmingly rural people. In the years that followed, there was a slow but steady migration of blacks to the cities, mainly in the South. Migration to the North was relatively small. Nearly eight million blacks—about 90 percent of the total black population of the United States—were still living in the South in 1900.

But between 1910 and 1920, crop damage caused by floods and insects—mainly the boll weevil—deepened an already severe economic depression in southern agriculture. Impoverished blacks swarmed to the North in 1915 and 1916, as thousands of new jobs opened up in industries supplying goods to Europe, then embroiled in World War I. Between 1910 and 1920, an estimated 500,000 blacks left the South, in what became known as the Great Migration.

In northern cities, blacks faced a new set of challenges. Many took on low-paying jobs. Additionally, many remained segregated from whites and lived in ghettos. However, blacks also had new economic and educational opportunities. Publications and organizations dedicated

After the panic of 1893, many property owners in Harlem began renting homes to blacks. By the 1920s, Harlem was known as an African American residential, commercial, and cultural center.

to helping migrant blacks also facilitated their adjustment to urban life.

The Great Migration helped set the social foundation for the later cultural movement known as the Harlem Renaissance, a blossoming of African American culture—particularly in the creative arts—and the most influential movement in African American literary history. The Harlem Renaissance was a phase of the larger New Negro movement that had emerged in the early 20th century and in some ways ushered in the early civil rights movement of the late 1940s and early 1950s.

Several factors contributed to the flourishing of this movement. First, levels of literacy among blacks were rising dramatically. Second, a number of national organizations dedicated to pressing African American civil rights, "uplifting" the race, and opening socioeconomic opportunities were established. Lastly, there was growing racial pride, which was encouraged by Pan-African programs and a growing sense of Pan-African ties. Black exiles and expatriates from the Caribbean and Africa crossed paths in cities such as New York City and Paris after World War I. There they had an invigorating influence on each other that made the broader "Negro renaissance" (as it was then known) profoundly important internationally.

The Harlem Renaissance lasted from c. 1918 to 1937. Participants embraced literary, musical, theatrical, and visual arts and sought to create a new "Negro" identity, apart from the white stereotypes that had influenced black peoples' relationship to their heritage and to each other. They also wanted to break free of Victorian moral values and shame about aspects of their lives that might, as seen by whites, reinforce racist beliefs. The movement was never dominated by a particular school of thought. Instead, it was characterized by intense debate. It laid the groundwork for all later African American literature and had an enormous impact on black consciousness worldwide. While the renaissance was not confined to the Harlem district of New York City, Harlem attracted a remarkable concentration of intellect and talent and served as the symbolic capital of this cultural awakening.

The Harlem Renaissance is unusual among literary and artistic movements for its close relationship to civil rights and reform organizations. But with the onset of the Great Depression, new economic realities took hold. African American artists and writers in the 1930s sought to distance themselves from their predecessors by creating works that were more politically and socially conscious. Still, the Harlem Renaissance left an important legacy. Black cultural figures became leading voices of the black experience and the arbiters of a new black identity. And their works started reaching—and influencing—increasingly wider audiences. The history of these remarkable periods is surveyed in the following pages.

CHAPTER ONE

ECONOMIC DEPRESSION AND THE MOVE NORTH

In 1900, the vast majority of African Americans lived in the southern states. From 1916 to 1970, during what is known as the Great Migration, about six million black southerners relocated to other parts of the country. Much of this resettlement took place between World Wars I and II. Most of the migrants moved from rural communities in the South to large cities in the North and West, including Chicago, New York, and Detroit, seeking greater economic opportunities and improved living conditions.

PUSH AND PULL FACTORS

In every migration, certain conditions motivate people to leave an area; these are known as push factors. Other conditions, the pull factors, attract people to the new area. In the Great Migration, the push factors included poor economic conditions in the South. After the American Civil War, slavery was ended in 1865. Lacking both money and land, many freed Southern blacks became sharecroppers, renting farmland from

Black sharecroppers pick cotton in Georgia in 1898. Poor economic conditions in the early 20th century led many such workers in the South to migrate to other areas of the United States.

white landowners by paying them a portion of their crops. The sharecropping system required grueling labor and supplied very low incomes. Between 1910 and 1920, an already severe economic depression in southern agriculture worsened. Crops were damaged by floods and insects, notably the boll weevil, and farms failed. Impoverished blacks began migrating away from the South in great numbers.

Another important factor that pushed African Americans to leave the South was ongoing racial oppression. The great majority of Southern whites remained fiercely opposed to African American political, civil, and social equality. The Southern states used a variety of means to keep blacks from voting. So-called Jim Crow laws enforced racial segregation in the South, preventing African Americans from using buses, schools, restaurants, theaters, and other facilities reserved for whites.

The pull factors in the Great Migration included encouraging reports of good living conditions and jobs with good wages in the North and West. Starting in the late 19th century, large numbers of Europeans had moved to the United States. With the onset of World War I and the introduction of a series of laws in the 1920s that greatly restricted immigration, fewer Europeans were available to provide cheap labor. As a result, urban industries were faced with labor shortages. An even greater number of jobs became available in the cities during World War I and World War II, when defense industries required more unskilled labor. Large numbers of African Americans moved to the northern cities to seek employment. Although the Great Migration slowed during the Great Depression, it surged again after World War II, when rates of migration were high for several decades.

THE *CHICAGO DEFENDER*

Founded in 1905 by Robert S. Abbott, the *Chicago Defender* originally was a four-page weekly newspaper. Like the white-owned Hearst and Pulitzer newspapers, the *Defender*, under Abbott, used sensationalism to boost circulation. Editorials attacking white oppression and the lynching of African Americans helped increase the paper's circulation in southern states. During World War I the *Defender* urged equal treatment of black soldiers. It published dispatches that contrasted opportunities for African Americans in the urban North with the hardships of the rural South. This contributed actively to the northward migration of millions of black southerners between World War I and the Great Depression. By 1929, the *Defender* was selling more than 250,000 copies each week.

A number of prominent black writers contributed to the *Defender*, including noted Harlem Renaissance poet and author Langston Hughes, who wrote a column for more than 20 years. His "Simple" stories first appeared in his column in 1942. Although its readership and influence has declined since the 1990s, the *Defender* remains in circulation.

NEW DIFFICULTIES

News of the better conditions for blacks in the North and West spread by word of mouth and by reports and advertisements in African American newspapers. The influential black newspaper the *Chicago Defender*, for example, became one of the leading promoters of the Great Migration. In addition to Chicago, Illinois, other cities that absorbed large numbers of black migrants

Blacks who migrated to northern and western cities found both new economic opportunities and new challenges. Many lived in ghettos such as this one in Chicago.

included Detroit, Michigan; Cleveland, Ohio; and New York, New York.

Seeking better civil and economic opportunities, many blacks were not wholly able to escape racism by migrating to the North. African Americans there were segregated into ghettos, where they lived in overcrowded and dilapidated housing, and urban life introduced new obstacles. They were also largely restricted to poorly paid, menial jobs. Newly arriving migrants even encountered social challenges from the black establishment in the North, which tended to look down on the "country" manners of the newcomers.

There were antiblack riots, such as that in East St. Louis, Illinois, in 1917. But in the northern cities the economic and educational opportunities for blacks were immeasurably greater than they had been in the rural South. In addition, they were helped by various organizations, such as the National Urban League, founded in 1910.

NATIONAL URBAN LEAGUE

The problems African Americans encountered in the cities—racial discrimination, substandard housing and education, and an unfamiliar way of life—led to the founding of the Committee on Urban Conditions Among Negroes in New York City on Sept. 29, 1910. The central figures in the establishment of the committee were Ruth Standish Baldwin, a white philanthropist, and George Edmund Haynes, a social worker and the first African American to earn a Ph.D. from New York's Columbia University. Their objectives were to help the migrants from the South adjust to urban living, to help train

George Edmund Haynes (*right*) served as the first executive secretary of the Committee on Urban Conditions Among Negroes, which would later merge with other organizations to become the National Urban League.

African American social workers, and to increase the opportunities available to African Americans for education and work.

In 1911, the committee merged with the Committee for the Improvement of Industrial Conditions Among Negroes in New York and with the National League for the Protection of Colored Women (both founded in 1906). The new organization, the National League on Urban Conditions Among Negroes, served as a model for affiliated groups in other cities. In 1920, it changed its name to the National Urban League. By the end of World War I, the organization was represented in 30 U.S. cities.

Under the direction of Eugene Kinckle Jones, who served as chairman from 1918 to 1941, the National Urban League expanded its efforts to integrate the U.S. workforce and labor unions. Jones's successor, Lester Granger, led the organization in the fight against discrimination in the armed services and armament factories during World War II. Building on these efforts, the league worked in the years after the war to convince large corporations to recruit on African American college campuses and to promote African Americans to high-level positions.

During the civil rights movement, the organization worked to improve the living conditions of African Americans. It continued to introduce new social services for blacks throughout the remainder of the 20th century and into the 21st.

WORLD WAR I

In 1917, the United States declared war against Germany and entered World War I on the side of the Allied forces. African Americans were divided on the subject of the fight for democracy in Europe. Some blacks opposed involvement in World War I. The

In New York City during World War I, the NAACP led a march protesting brutality against African Americans. One of the many banners read, "Mr. President, why not make America safe for democracy?"

black Socialists A. Philip Randolph and Chandler Owen argued that the fight for democracy—and civil rights—at home should precede the fight for it abroad.

But when the United States entered World War I in April 1917, most blacks supported the step. Many viewed it as their patriotic duty to serve the war effort. Some black leaders saw African Americans' contributions to the war as a step toward improved civil rights. By serving their country and demonstrating that their commitment to democracy was equal to that of whites, many blacks felt that they would finally be treated as equal citizens. During the war about 1,400 black officers were commissioned. Some 200,000 blacks served abroad, though most were restricted to labor battalions and service regiments.

Many African Americans became disillusioned following World War I. The jobs that they had acquired during the war all but evaporated in the post-war recession, which hit African Americans first and hardest. The Ku Klux Klan, which had been revived during the war, unleashed a new wave of terror against blacks. Mounting competition for jobs and housing often erupted into bloody "race riots" such as those that spread over the nation in the "Red Summer" of 1919. And the civil rights that African Americans had hoped to gain following the war were nowhere in sight.

THE RED SUMMER

During the summer of 1919, racial tensions between white and black Americans erupted into a series of violent and deadly riots throughout the United States. This period, named the Red Summer by black leaders, witnessed twenty-six race riots in which hundreds of people, mostly African American, were killed or injured.

The rioting began in early July in a small town in Texas and soon spread to nearly every major city in the United States, including Washington, D.C. and Omaha, Nebraska. One of the most violent disturbances began in Chicago, Ill., in late July when Eugene Williams, a black teenager, was drowned by whites throwing rocks after he swam near the white side of a segregated beach. After the police refused to arrest those who had thrown the rocks, fighting broke out and quickly engulfed the city. The rioting lasted five days, leaving 38 people dead and more than 500 injured. Extensive property damage, particularly to black sections of the city, left an estimated 1,000 African Americans homeless. The pressure for adequate housing on the South Side of Chicago was a driving factor of the racial tension there: the black population had increased from 44,000 in 1910 to more than 109,000 in 1920.

Another notable disturbance took place in the rural area around Elaine, Arkansas, where black farmers

White children raid an African American home during the Chicago Race Riot of 1919. Blacks both in Chicago and throughout the country contended with many acts of aggression, violence, and vandalism throughout the Red Summer.

were attempting to form a union. Official reports put the death toll at 30, including 25 blacks, but the true count may have exceeded 100.

The horror of the Red Summer helped shock the nation out of indifference to its growing racial conflict. Pres. Woodrow Wilson criticized the "white race" as "the aggressor" in both the Chicago and Washington riots, and efforts were launched to promote racial harmony through voluntary organizations and ameliorative legislation in Congress. The period also marked a new willingness on the part of black men to fight for their rights in the face of injustice and oppression.

CHAPTER TWO

THE BIRTH OF THE HARLEM RENAISSANCE

In the face of the difficulties following World War I, a "new Negro" developed during the 1920s—the proud, creative product of the American city. The growth of racial pride among African Americans was greatly stimulated by the black nationalist ideas of Marcus Garvey as well as those of such thinkers as W. E. B. Du Bois. Garvey was a proponent of Pan-Africanism, the idea that peoples of African descent have common interests and should be unified. Although he was not the first to espouse Pan-Africanist ideals, he was instrumental in galvanizing the first major black nationalist movement in the United States and in the creation of a new black identity.

Marcus Garvey is shown chairing a session of the Universal Negro Improvement Association, 1924.

PAN-AFRICANISM AND BLACK NATIONALISM

Born in Jamaica, Marcus Garvey had founded the Universal Negro Improvement Association (UNIA) there in 1914. He came to the United States in 1917 and established a branch of the association in the Harlem district of New York City. By 1919 the association had become the largest mass movement of American blacks in the nation's history, with a membership of several hundred thousand.

The Garvey movement was characterized by colorful pageantry and appeals for the rediscovery of the black African heritage. Its goal was to establish an independent Africa through the return of a revolutionary vanguard of black Americans. Garvey's great attraction among poor blacks was not matched, however, among the black middle class, which resented his flamboyance and his scorn of their leadership.

Indeed, one of Garvey's sharpest critics was W. E. B. Du Bois, who shared Garvey's basic goals. Du Bois's black nationalism took several forms. He organized a series of small but largely ineffectual Pan-African conferences during the 1920s. Additionally, as the editor of *The Crisis*, he encouraged the development of black literature and art and urged his readers to see "Beauty in Black." Du Bois's black nationalism is also evident in his belief that blacks should develop a separate "group economy" in which black producers and consumers would operate independently of the white economy. He believed this would help fight economic discrimination and black poverty.

UNIVERSAL NEGRO IMPROVEMENT ASSOCIATION

The Universal Negro Improvement Association (UNIA) was founded by Marcus Garvey and dedicated to racial pride, economic self-sufficiency, and the formation of an independent black nation in Africa. Though Garvey had founded the UNIA in Jamaica in 1914, its main influence was felt in the principal urban black neighborhoods of the U.S. North after his arrival in Harlem, in New York City, in 1916.

Garvey had a strong appeal to poor blacks in urban ghettos, but most black leaders in the United States criticized him as an imposter, particularly after he announced, in New York, the founding of the Empire of Africa, with himself as provisional president. In turn, Garvey denounced the National Association for the Advancement of Colored People (NAACP) and many black leaders, asserting that they sought only assimilation into white society. Garvey's leadership was cut short in 1923 when he was indicted and convicted of fraud in his handling of funds raised to establish a black steamship line. In 1927, President Calvin Coolidge pardoned Garvey but ordered him deported as an undesirable alien.

The UNIA never revived. Although the organization did not transport a single person to Africa, its influence reached multitudes on both sides of the Atlantic, and it proved to be a forerunner of the black nationalism that emerged in the United States after World War II.

Although Pan-Africanist and black nationalist thinking endured in various forms over the next several decades, the Garvey movement declined after Garvey was jailed for mail fraud in 1925 and was deported to Jamaica in 1927.

A NEW CULTURAL CENTER

Before the 1920s, African American culture was unknown or unrecognized by most white Americans. Buoyed by a new confidence and racial pride, however, African American writers, artists, and musicians came together in Harlem in the 1920s to leverage the power of art as an agent of change. Their sophisticated explorations of their life and culture became the hallmarks of the Harlem Renaissance. Like the Garvey movement, the Harlem Renaissance was based on a rise in race consciousness among blacks. For the first time, they succeeded in bringing serious critical consideration and respect to African American arts and ideas.

The renaissance had many sources in black culture, primarily of the United States and the Caribbean, and manifested itself well beyond Harlem. As its symbolic capital, Harlem was a catalyst for artistic experimentation and a highly popular nightlife destination. Its location in the communications capital of North America helped give the "New Negroes" visibility and opportunities for publication not evident elsewhere. Located just north of Central Park, Harlem was a formerly white residential district that by the early 1920s was becoming virtually a black city within

Displays of Harlem's vibrant creative culture could be seen in its bustling nightlife. Numerous popular dance crazes were launched by the patrons of the Savoy Ballroom, a large music and dance hall, which opened in Harlem in 1926 and drew black and white crowds alike.

the borough of Manhattan. Other boroughs of New York City were also home to people now identified with the renaissance, but they often crossed paths in Harlem or went to special events at the 135th Street Branch of the New York Public Library. Black intellectuals from Washington, Baltimore, Philadelphia, Los Angeles, and other cities (where they had their own intellectual circles, theaters, and reading groups) also met in Harlem or settled there. New York City had an extraordinarily diverse and decentralized black social world in which no one group could monopolize cultural authority. As a result, it was a particularly fertile place for cultural experimentation.

Philosopher Alain Locke proclaimed the movement in *The New Negro* (1925), in which he called the northward migration of African Americans to urban centers in the 1910s and 1920s "something like a spiritual emancipation." W. E. B. Du Bois and James Weldon Johnson joined Locke in urging blacks to celebrate their African heritage and explore new modes of self-expression.

The principal contributors to the Harlem Renaissance included not only well-established literary figures

ALAIN LOCKE

Alain LeRoy Locke was born in Philadelphia, Pennsylvania, on September 13, 1886. Both his parents were schoolteachers. They wanted their son to enter a profession like medicine, as a means of rising above some of the restrictions that were placed upon his race. But sickness made a career as a doctor

Alain LeRoy Locke was an educator, writer, and philosopher, best remembered as the leader and chief interpreter of the Harlem Renaissance.

impossible, and his parents helped young Locke to prepare himself as a teacher.

Locke graduated with a degree in philosophy from Harvard University (1907) and became the first black Rhodes scholar, studying at Oxford (1907–10) and the University of Berlin (1910–11). He received his Ph.D. in philosophy from Harvard (1918). He taught at Howard University in Washington, D.C., for nearly 40 years.

Locke stimulated and guided artistic activities and promoted the recognition and respect of blacks by the broader American community. Having studied African culture and traced its influences upon Western civilization, he urged black painters, sculptors, and musicians to look to African sources for identity and to discover materials and techniques for their work. He encouraged black authors to seek subjects in black life and to set high artistic standards for themselves. He familiarized American readers with the Harlem Renaissance by editing a special Harlem issue for *Survey Graphic* (March 1925), which he expanded into his first book, *The New Negro* (1925).

Locke's books stressed black culture, but he always tried to show how this fitted into the whole of American life. He acted either as author or editor for a number of titles. He left unfinished materials for a definitive study of the contributions of blacks to American culture. Locke died in New York City on June 9, 1954.

such as Du Bois and the poet James Weldon Johnson but also new young writers such as Claude McKay, who penned the poem "If We Must Die," one of the most quoted black literary works of this period. Other outstanding writers of the Harlem Renaissance were

THE CRISIS

A RECORD OF THE DARKER RACES

| Volume One | NOVEMBER, 1910 | Number One |

Edited by W. E. BURGHARDT DU BOIS, with the co-operation of Oswald Garrison Villard, J. Max Barber, Charles Edward Russell, Kelly Miller, W. S. Braithwaite and M. D. Maclean.

CONTENTS

PUBLISHED MONTHLY BY THE

National Association for the Advancement of Colored People

AT TWENTY VESEY STREET   NEW YORK CITY

ONE DOLLAR A YEAR   TEN CENTS A COPY

The Crisis: A Record of the Darker Races was a monthly magazine, edited by W. E. B. Du Bois for 24 years, that published the works of many young black writers. The cover of the first issue from 1910 is pictured here.

the novelist Jean Toomer and the poets Countee Cullen and Langston Hughes.

During the 1920s, the artists Henry Ossawa Tanner and Aaron Douglas and the performers Paul Robeson, Florence Mills, Ethel Waters, and Roland Hayes were also becoming prominent. The black cultural movement of the 1920s was greatly stimulated by black journals, which published short pieces by promising writers. These journals included the NAACP's *Crisis* and the National Urban League's *Opportunity*. *Negro World*, the newspaper of Garvey's UNIA, also played a role, but few of the major authors or artists identified with Garvey's "Back to Africa" movement, even if they contributed to the paper.

CHAPTER THREE

A LITERARY MOVEMENT

The phenomenon known as the Harlem Renaissance represented the flowering in literature and art of the New Negro movement of the 1920s. It was epitomized in Alain Locke's anthology *The New Negro* (1925), which featured the early work of some of the most gifted Harlem Renaissance writers, including the poets Countee Cullen, Langston Hughes, and Claude McKay and the novelists Rudolph Fisher, Zora Neale Hurston, and Jean Toomer.

The "New Negro," Locke announced, differed from the "Old Negro" in assertiveness and self-confidence, which led New Negro writers to question traditional "white" artistic standards, to reject narrow viewpoints and propaganda, and to cultivate

Even before he finished college, Countee Cullen had published a critically acclaimed collection of poems, *Color* (1925). He became known as one of the finest poets of the Harlem Renaissance.

personal self-expression, racial pride, and literary experimentation. Major American magazines, book publishers, and white patrons took an unprecedented interest in black writing, which spurred the success of writers of the Harlem Renaissance. Many black writers received positive critical reviews and financial rewards—a trend that lasted, at least for a few, until well into the Great Depression of the 1930s.

POETRY

Claude McKay is generally regarded as the first major poet of the Harlem Renaissance. His best poetry, including sonnets ranging from the militant "If We Must Die" (1919) to the brooding self-portrait "Outcast," was collected in *Harlem Shadows* (1922). Some critics have called it the first great literary achievement of the Harlem Renaissance. Poet Langston Hughes admired McKay but preferred to write free verse, in the style of Walt Whitman and Carl Sandburg. Hughes also found ways to write in an African American street vernacular that evokes a broad range of moods and emotions. Hughes earned his

r his poem, "The Negro Speaks of Rivers,"
th a radio program. Yale University Library

A poem by Langston Hughes is displayed at the African American Heritage Museum of Southern New Jersey. Hughes remains widely regarded as one of the foremost interpreters to the world of the black experience in the United States.

greatest praise for his experimental jazz and blues poetry in *The Weary Blues* (1926) and *Fine Clothes to the Jew* (1927). While McKay and Hughes proudly identified themselves as black poets, Countee Cullen sought success through writing in traditional forms, inspired by the work of John Keats. Cullen's

LANGSTON HUGHES

Known during his lifetime as the poet laureate of Harlem, Langston Hughes also worked as a journalist, dramatist, and children's author. His poems, which tell of the joys and miseries of the ordinary black man in America, have been widely translated.

James Langston Hughes was born on February 1, 1902, in Joplin, Missouri. When he was still a baby, his parents separated, and his father went to Mexico. Hughes lived in Lawrence, Kansas, where his grandmother helped rear him. After she died, he and his mother eventually moved to Cleveland, Ohio, where he wrote poems for his high school's magazine. After graduating, he went to Mexico for a year or so to be with his father. In 1921, he enrolled at Columbia University in New York City, but he was so lonely and unhappy that he left after a year.

He then explored Harlem, forming a permanent attachment to what he called the "great dark city." He later worked various jobs. His first book of poetry, *The Weary Blues*, published in 1926, made him known among literary people. He went to Lincoln University in Oxford, Pennsylvania, on a scholarship and received his B.A. degree there in 1929.

From then on, Hughes earned his living as a writer, portraying African American life with idiomatic realism. *Not*

Langston Hughes stands on a street in Harlem. Although he left New York for part of the 1920s, he would return and spend much of the rest of his life in Harlem.

Without Laughter, a novel published in 1930, won the Harmon gold medal for literature. A book of poems for children, *The Dream Keeper*, came out in 1932. His play *Mulatto* opened on Broadway in 1935. He wrote the lyrics for *Street Scene*, a 1947 opera by Kurt Weill. Hughes also lectured in schools and colleges, where he talked with black youth who had literary ability and encouraged them to write.

In the 1950s and 1960s, Hughes's work included a volume of poetry, a book of short stories, and a children's picture book. Hughes died in New York City on May 22, 1967.

ambivalence about racial identification as a man or a poet is evident in his most famous poem, "Heritage" (1925).

PROSE

McKay and Hughes made names for themselves in prose as well. McKay's novel *Home to Harlem* (1928) earned a substantial readership, especially among those curious about the more lurid side of Harlem's nightlife. Hughes's autobiography, *The Big Sea* (1940), contains the most insightful and unsentimental first-person account of the Harlem Renaissance ever published. Yet the most notable narratives produced by the Harlem Renaissance came from Jean Toomer (himself an accomplished poet), Rudolph Fisher, Wallace Thurman, Zora Neale Hurston, and Nella Larsen.

Toomer's *Cane* (1923) is an experimental novel that presents African American life in rural Georgia and in the urban North; it is regarded as one of the most significant works of African American literature. Fisher's *The Walls of Jericho* (1928) won critical applause because of the novel's balanced satire of class and color prejudice among black New Yorkers. In 1932, Fisher brought out *The Conjure Man Dies*, often referred to as the first African American detective novel. Thurman's *The Blacker the Berry* (1929) exposes color prejudice among African Americans and is among the first African American novels to address the topic of homosexuality. The struggles and frustrations Larsen revealed in the black female protagonists of her novels *Quicksand* (1928) and *Passing* (1929) likely speak to the problems

Noted Harlem Renaissance artist Aaron Douglas designed the dust jacket for Claude McKay's book *A Long Way from Home* (1937).

Larsen herself faced as a sophisticated New Negro woman trying to find her own way in the supposedly liberated racial and sexual atmosphere of the 1920s.

Like Toomer, Larsen fell silent after the Harlem Renaissance. The early short stories of Hurston appeared in the late 1920s, and of the major fiction writers of the Harlem Renaissance, she was the only one who published a masterwork after its end. Her second novel guaranteed her permanent reputation among African American novelists. In *Their Eyes Were Watching God* (1937), Hurston's protagonist, Janie Crawford, embodies the ethos of a vibrant working-class southern black

ZORA NEALE HURSTON

Writer, folklorist, and anthropologist Zora Neale Hurston celebrated the African American culture of the rural South. She wrote several novels as well as books of black mythology, legends, and folklore.

Hurston was born on January 7, 1891, in Notasulga, Alabama. She moved with her family to Eatonville, Florida, as a small child. When she was 16 years old, she joined a traveling theater company and ended up in New York City during the Harlem Renaissance. Hurston attended Howard University from 1921 to 1924 and in 1925 won a scholarship to Barnard College, where she studied anthropology. She graduated from Barnard in 1928 and for two years pursued graduate studies in anthropology at Columbia University. She also conducted field studies in folklore among African Americans in the South. One result of these studies was the book *Mules and Men* (1935), a collection of folklore presented within the framework of a unifying narrative.

Zora Neale Hurston beats a Haitian hountar, or mama drum. Hurston wrote *Their Eyes Were Watching God* while studying Haitian folklore and culture.

Hurston's background was also reflected in her novels, most of which incorporated elements of folklore to some degree. After studying in Haiti and Jamaica in 1936, she wrote *Their Eyes Were Watching God* (1937), which is widely considered her finest novel. It tells the story of a young black woman's growth toward self-awareness and independence. Hurston's other novels are *Jonah's Gourd Vine* (1934), *Moses, Man of the Mountain* (1939), and *Seraph on the Suwanee* (1948). She collaborated with Langston Hughes on the play *Mule Bone* (1931).

Hurston served on the faculty of North Carolina College for Negroes (now North Carolina Central University) in Durham. She also worked at the Library of Congress. By the time of her death Hurston was little remembered by the general reading public, but there was a resurgence of interest in her work in the late 20th century. Several other collections were published posthumously. Hurston died on Jan. 28, 1960, in Fort Pierce, Florida.

community. Her sassy tongue and heroic reclaiming of herself make Janie Crawford the greatest single literary character created by the New Negro generation.

DRAMA

Although the most memorable literary achievement of the Harlem Renaissance was in narrative prose and poetry, the movement also inspired great works of drama. Blackface minstrelsy had created a powerful range of damaging stereotypes that presented a false view of black life in theater. Drama of the Harlem Renaissance sought to overcome the decades-long influence of such stereotypes on the popular imagination. Critics, playwrights, and actors debated the function of drama, as well as its subject matter and the style of presentation of "Negro experience." A number of white-authored plays about black life gained great critical and box-office success from the late 1910s through the mid-1930s, giving valuable experience to black performers and inspiring

Performers of the Lafayette Theater in Harlem—known as the Lafayette Players—pose for a photograph. The venue drew black and white audiences and raised the profile of black actors who often assumed serious roles intended for white actors.

black dramatists. Black playwrights were moved to present more authentic examples of what were called Negro plays. New all-black theater groups arose in several cities.

Hurston's plays drew on her vast firsthand knowledge of rural Southern folklore and freely used humor and exaggeration in depicting everyday black life. Some of her short plays made it to Broadway after being incorporated into the musicals *Fast and Furious* (first performed 1931) and *The Great Day* (first performed 1932). Wallace Thurman cowrote with William Jourdan Rapp the successful and somewhat controversial play *Harlem* (1929), a fast-paced slice of Harlem life, notable for its vernacular and slang-filled dialogue. Most successful of all the black-written plays of the Harlem Renaissance was Hughes's *Mulatto* (written 1931, first performed 1935); adapted from his short story "Father and Son," the play is set on a plantation in Georgia and concerns the tragic consequences of a white man's inability to acknowledge his only children because they are mulatto.

CHAPTER FOUR

VISUAL AND PERFORMING ARTS

Although it is remembered primarily as a literary movement, the Harlem Renaissance was a period of intense creativity in music and the visual arts as well. Outside of literature, artists such as Henry Ossawa Tanner and Aaron Douglas and performers such as Paul Robeson and Josephine Baker made their mark on the cultural landscape.

VISUAL ART

Visual artists of the Harlem Renaissance, like the dramatists, attempted to win control over representation

One of Aaron Douglas's most famous works, *Aspects of Negro Life* (1934), a four-panel series, uses elements of African art and culture to depict the African American journey from Africa to post–Civil War city life. This panel is titled *The Negro in an African Setting.*

of their people while developing a new repertoire of images. Prior to World War I, black painters and sculptors had rarely concerned themselves with African American subject matter. Representation of black life in the visual arts had generally been characterized by white caricature and denigration. By the end of the 1920s, however, black artists had begun developing styles related to black aesthetic traditions of Africa or to folk art.

The signature artist of the renaissance was Aaron Douglas, who turned away from traditional landscape painting after moving to New York City from Kansas and studying under the German immigrant Winold Reiss. His first major commission—to illustrate Alain Locke's book *The New Negro* (1925)—quickly prompted requests for graphics from other writers of the Harlem Renaissance, including Langston Hughes, Charles S. Johnson, Countee Cullen, Wallace Thurman, and James Weldon Johnson.

Douglas incorporated cubist forms with stylized and geometric shapes drawn from African art. He used the rhythm of circles, diagonals, and wavy lines to energize his illustrations. Through these techniques, he addressed the aspirations of the "New Negro" and depicted the realities of

Though often criticized for depicting caricatured black figures in his works, as seen here in his *Nous Quatre à Paris* (*We Four in Paris*) (1928–30), Palmer C. Hayden remained a highly regarded artist.

the black struggle for political and creative freedom. In addition to illustrations, Douglas made murals, including a series for the campus library at Fisk University in Nashville (1930).

Despite Douglas's importance, most black artists of the 1920s spent little time in Harlem. Paris was the mecca of black painters and sculptors in that decade. Yet traveling exhibits and contests in the United States encouraged black artists in the late 1920s and early '30s. Notable figures include the painter Palmer C. Hayden, who interpreted black folklore and working-class life; Archibald J. Motley, best known for his paintings of urban black social life and his realistic portraits of refined "New Negro" types; Augusta Savage and Richmond Barthé, both sculptors; and other visual artists such as Sargent Johnson, William H. Johnson, Hale Woodruff, Lois Mailou Jones, and James VanDerZee.

JAMES VANDERZEE

James VanDerZee was an American photographer, whose portraits chronicled the Harlem Renaissance. VanDerZee was born in Lenox, Massachusetts, in 1886. By 1906 he had moved with his father and brother to Harlem in New York City, where he worked as a waiter and elevator operator. In 1915 VanDerZee moved to Newark, New Jersey, where he took a job in a portrait studio, first as a darkroom assistant and then as a portraitist. He returned to Harlem the following year, setting up a portrait studio at a music conservatory that his sister had founded in 1911.

(continued on page 51)

This photograph by James VanDerZee, entitled *Future Expectations*, was made in 1925. VanDerZee worked predominantly in the studio and used various elements, including backdrops and costumes, to keep with late Victorian and Edwardian visual traditions.

(continued from page 49)

In 1916, VanDerZee and his second wife launched the Guarantee Photo Studio in Harlem. His business boomed during World War I, and the portraits he shot from this period until 1945 have demanded the majority of the critical attention devoted to him. Among his many renowned subjects were Countee Cullen, dancer Bill ("Bojangles") Robinson, and Marcus Garvey. Sitters often copied celebrities of the 1920s and '30s in their poses and expressions, and VanDerZee retouched negatives and prints heavily to achieve an aura of glamour.

After World War II, VanDerZee's fortunes declined with those of the rest of Harlem. His collection of negatives and prints was discovered by a representative of the Metropolitan Museum of Art in New York in 1967. By that time, the VanDerZees were nearly destitute. In early 1969 his photos were featured as part of the museum's successful "Harlem on My Mind" exhibition, which showcased life during the Harlem Renaissance in a variety of media. VanDerZee won increasing attention throughout the 1970s and worked until his death in 1983.

Many of these artists produced their best work in the 1930s and helped cultivate the next generation. The Great Depression forced many artists to return "home" from Europe and brought them together in a critical mass previously unknown. New York City became in the 1930s a center of art education with new galleries, schools, and museums, including the Museum of Modern Art, which had been founded in 1929. Most important for aspiring black artists were the School of Arts and Crafts, founded by Savage, and the Harlem Community Art Center, of which Savage

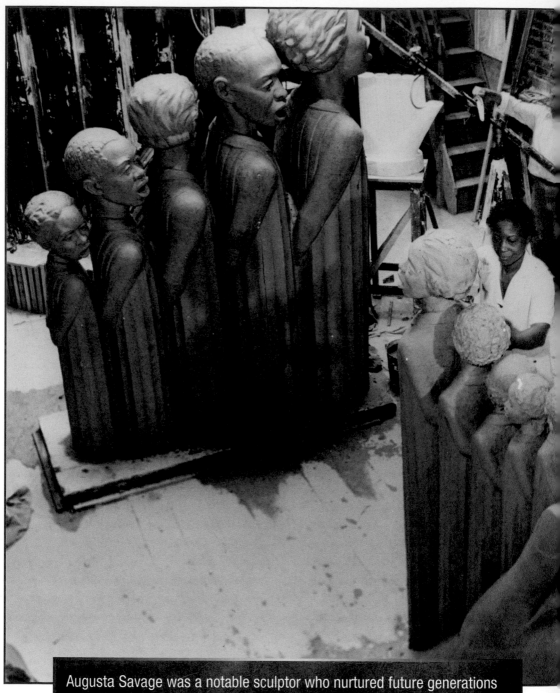

Augusta Savage was a notable sculptor who nurtured future generations of black artists and helped advance the place of black females in the art world. Here she is seen with her work *The Harp* (1939).

served as the first director after its creation in 1937 with Works Progress Administration (WPA) aid. In the middle and late 1930s, federal arts projects under the New Deal provided an unprecedented level of encouragement to the development of black artists and helped start the careers of a new generation of artists that included Romare Bearden, Jacob Lawrence, and Norman Lewis.

PERFORMING ARTS

In the 1920s, jazz became identified as an African American music tradition that had grown into a sophisticated modern art from its roots as folk music in the South. Jazz had international appeal, a connection to common black life, and boasted highly skilled musicians. This encouraged black intellectuals in other fields to turn increasingly to specifically "Negro" aesthetic forms as a basis for innovation and self-expression. The tendency appeared in concert music, choral programs, and Broadway musicals. Eubie Blake and Noble Sissle's musical revue *Shuffle Along* opened on Broadway in 1921 and established a model that would shape black musicals for 60 years. Florence Mills, a spritely dancer and

Florence Mills was a multitalented entertainer, capturing audiences with her singing, dancing, comedy, and acting. Although she died at 31, her popularity helped African American performers secure a place in mainstream theater.

phenomenal singer, achieved enormous fame across racial lines in the United States and Europe before suddenly succumbing to appendicitis in 1927. Dancer and singer Josephine Baker, who began as a chorus girl in a popular revue, became an international star when *La Revue Nègre* opened in 1925 in Paris, where she ultimately settled as a celebrity. Singer and actor Paul Robeson's appearance in the title role of playwright Eugene O'Neill's *The Emperor Jones* caused a sensation in New York City (1924) and London (1925). In 1925, Robeson also gave his first vocal recital of African American spirituals in Greenwich Village, New York City, and he became world famous as Joe in the musical *Show Boat* with his version of "Ol' Man River."

Popular revues and vaudeville acts drew all-black audiences throughout the United States in cities on the Theatre Owners Booking Association circuit. In the 1920s black-produced shows came to Broadway again and again, and many white-produced shows featured black casts. The success of such shows helped fuel the optimism of the Harlem Renaissance. Amid worsening socioeconomic conditions in Harlem itself and political setbacks in what was a very conservative and racist era—it was during the 1920s that the Ku Klux Klan reached its peak in membership and political influence in the South and the Midwest—some black leaders hoped that achievement in the arts would help revolutionize race relations while enhancing blacks' understanding of themselves as a people.

CHAPTER FIVE

THE GREAT DEPRESSION AND THE NEW DEAL

D espite the enormous outpouring of creativity during the 1920s, the vogue of black writing, black art, and black culture waned significantly in the early 1930s as the Great Depression took hold in the United States. The Great Depression worsened the already bleak economic situation of black Americans. Again the first to be laid off from their jobs, they suffered from an unemployment rate two to three times that of whites. In early public assistance programs, blacks often received substantially less aid than whites, and some charitable organizations even excluded blacks from their soup kitchens.

Workers, many of them migrants, grade beans at a canning plant in Florida in 1937. The economic hardships of the Great Depression hit African American workers especially hard.

Life in Harlem, as in many urban settings, was difficult during the 1930s. The once-teeming nightclubs that had employed so many blacks closed, and thousands of southern blacks, hoping to escape poverty and discrimination, settled in Harlem. To add to the residents' frustration, the New York City government generally neglected Harlem, so its streets, playgrounds, and public facilities were often the last on the list to be repaired. African American writers responded to these changing realities by distancing themselves from the works of the cultural figures of the Harlem Renaissance.

ECONOMIC AND POLITICAL STRUGGLES

Their intensified economic plight sparked major political developments among blacks. Beginning in 1929, the St. Louis Urban League launched a national "jobs for Negroes" movement by boycotting chain stores that had mostly black customers but hired only white employees. Efforts to unify black organizations and youth groups later led to the founding of the National Negro Congress in 1936 and the Southern Negro Youth Congress in 1937.

Virtually ignored by the Republican administrations of the 1920s, black voters drifted to the Democratic Party, especially in the Northern cities. In the presidential election of 1928, blacks voted in large numbers for the Democrats for the first time. In 1930 Republican President Herbert Hoover nominated John J. Parker, a man of pronounced antiblack views, to the U.S. Supreme Court. The NAACP successfully opposed the nomination. In the 1932 presidential race, blacks overwhelmingly supported the successful Democratic candidate, Franklin D. Roosevelt.

THE NEW DEAL

The Roosevelt administration's accessibility to black leaders and the New Deal reforms strengthened black support for the Democratic Party. Many black leaders, members of a so-called "black cabinet," were advisers to Roosevelt. Among them were the educator Mary McLeod Bethune, who served as the National Youth Administration's director of Negro affairs; William H. Hastie, who in 1937 became the first black federal judge; Eugene K. Jones, executive secretary of the National Urban League; Robert Vann, editor of the *Pittsburgh Courier*; and the economist Robert C. Weaver.

MARY MCLEOD BETHUNE

Mary Jane McLeod Bethune was a pioneer in African American education in the United States. She was born on July 10, 1875, in Mayesville, South Carolina, the first member of her family to be born free. As a child she worked in her parents' cotton fields. When an African American missionary opened a small school in Mayesville, only one person from the family could be spared from the fields to attend. The chosen one, Mary was able to continue her education at Scotia Seminary in Concord, North Carolina, and the Moody Bible Institute in Chicago, Illinois.

From 1895 to 1903 Mary McLeod taught in mission schools for African Americans in the South. In 1898 she married Albert Bethune, a teacher. In 1904 she rented a shack in Daytona Beach, Florida, and opened the Daytona Educational and Training School. Her son, Albert, was the only boy enrolled.

Within two years, however, she had 250 pupils. Most of them were girls, since she felt that African American girls

(continued on the next page)

(continued from the previous page)

were particularly hampered by lack of opportunities for improvement. The school was so successful that in 1923 it merged with Cookman Institute, a nearby men's college, and in 1929 the school was renamed Bethune-Cookman College. Her efforts for improved racial relations and African American education brought her the Spingarn Medal in 1935. Under President Franklin D. Roosevelt, she headed the Division of Negro Affairs of the National Youth Administration and was an adviser on African American affairs.

Bethune received many honorary degrees. She was an officer of numerous organizations, including the National Council of Negro Women, which she founded in 1935. After serving under Roosevelt from 1936 to 1943, she was a special assistant to the secretary of war during World War II. She died on May 18, 1955, in Daytona Beach.

Throughout her career, Mary McLeod Bethune worked to advance the rights of African Americans—especially African American children and women—and secure greater opportunities for them.

Blacks benefited greatly from New Deal programs, though discrimination by local administrators was common. Low-cost public housing was made available to black families. The National Youth Administration and the Civilian Conservation Corps enabled black youths to continue their education. The Works Progress Administration gave jobs to many blacks, and its Federal Writers' Project supported the work of many authors, among them Zora Neale Hurston, Arna Bontemps, Waters Turpin, and Melvin B. Tolson.

The Congress of Industrial Organizations (CIO), established in the mid-1930s, organized large numbers of black workers into labor unions for the first time. By 1940 there were more than 200,000 blacks in the CIO, many of them officers of union locals.

BLACK CHICAGO RENAISSANCE

African American pundits in the 1930s and '40s tended to depreciate the achievements of the New Negroes, calling instead for a more politically engaged, socially critical realism in literature. The chief proponent of this position was Richard Wright, whose fiction, autobiography, and social commentary dominated African American literature from the late 1930s to the early 1950s. His writings speak with the raw voice of an anguish not often evident in novels.

A migrant from Mississippi with barely a ninth-grade education, Wright set the tone for the post-New Negro era with *Uncle Tom's Children* (1938), a collection of novellas set in the Jim Crow South that evidenced Wright's strong affinity with Marxism and the influence of American naturalist writers such as Theodore

John L. Lewis was the founder and first president of the Congress of Industrial Organizations (CIO), a federation of unions that organized black labor during the Great Depression.

Dreiser. In 1940, Wright's monumental novel *Native Son*—charting the violent life and death of a Chicago ghetto youth—appeared, winning thunderous critical acclaim as well as unprecedented financial success. Wright's autobiography *Black Boy* (1945) revisited the 19th-century tradition of the slave narrative to chronicle his quest—as much intellectual as physical—from an oppressive South to anticipated freedom in Chicago. The stamp Wright placed on African American prose remained evident in the work of novelists such as William Attaway, Chester Himes, and Ann Petry, who have often been interpreted as belonging to "the Wright school" of social realism. Petry's *The Street* (1946) adopted Wright's pitiless assessment of the power of environment in the lives of black urban dwellers. However, unlike Wright, whose female characters generally exemplify demoralization and passivity, Petry created a female protagonist who fights back.

The *Chicago Defender* portrayed the Windy City as a cultural and economic mecca for black migrants fleeing the South during the Great Depression. Wright, who moved from Memphis, Tennessee, to Chicago in 1927, found in the South Side of Chicago a lively community of young African American writers, among them poet Margaret Walker, playwright Theodore Ward, poet and journalist Frank Marshall Davis, and novelist and children's book author Arna Bontemps. Chicago-based *Abbott's Monthly* (1930–33) published the work of Wright and Himes for the first time, while *New Challenge* (1937), coedited by novelist Dorothy West and Wright, helped the fledgling Chicago black literary renaissance develop. In the 1940s, *Negro Digest* and *Negro Story*, also literary products of Chicago's South Side, provided outlets for fiction

Richard Wright's socially and politically engaged works launched a new black renaissance on Chicago's South Side. Wright founded the South Side Writers Group, a writing circle whose members included numerous other black authors.

writers, poets, and essayists. Encouraged by the Chicago and New York units of the Federal Theater Project, African American drama advanced during the Depression, led by Abram Hill, founder of the American Negro Theater in Harlem; Hughes, whose play *Mulatto* (produced 1935) reached Broadway with a searching examination of miscegenation; and Ward, whose *Big White Fog* (produced 1938) was the most widely viewed African American drama of the period.

Archibald Motley was a Harlem Renaissance artist who was inspired by the nightlife, especially the jazz music, he found in Chicago's Bronzeville neighborhood. This painting is entitled *The Jazz Singers* (1934).

Artists such as Archibald J. Motley and numerous jazz and blues musicians also thrived in Chicago during this period.

The sobering realities of the Great Depression had engendered a more politically engaged generation of writers and artists. Yet although the cultural activity that in the 1930s swept the South Side of Chicago—in the neighborhood now called Bronzeville—lacked some of the optimistic spirit of the renaissance in Harlem, it owed much to the earlier movement. Together, they challenged traditional thinking about race and culture and set the stage for the civil rights gains made in the following decades.

CONCLUSION

A s blacks flocked to industrial centers beginning in 1915, they increasingly competed with whites for jobs, housing, and union wages. This migration created both new opportunities and new difficulties. Increased racial consciousness, with its roots in economic and civil rights struggles, eventually gave way to one of the most vibrant periods of creativity in African American history. Once home to a number of New York's prominent families, Harlem by the early 1900s had become a major center of African American culture and provided the backdrop against which the Harlem Renaissance was set. By the 1930s African Americans had begun to make some strides toward equality—the first African American since Reconstruction had been elected to Congress; boycotts had resulted in opening up job opportunities for African Americans; and the Congress of Industrial Organizations had become the first union to admit blacks.

Despite those steps, however, racial inequality was still prevalent. The Great Depression had left the national economy in shambles. Millions of people, of all ethnicities, were out of work. Further,

African Americans continued to be the victims of discriminatory practices. They were often the first to be fired and the last to be hired. As homeowners they struggled with redlining policies, unfair rents, and falling property values. As World War II approached, blacks again started leaving the South in large numbers in search of opportunities in larger Northern cities. As competition for housing and jobs escalated, so too did racial tensions. It was not until after the end of that war that blacks finally began seeing greater gains in their efforts towards racial equality.

African American literature and art from these later periods reflected the changing realities of black and urban life. However, even as African American writers of the 1930s attempted to differentiate their work from that of what was known then as the "Harlem movement" of the previous decade, it became clear that many of their works owed much to the experiments of such writers of the previous generation as Hurston, McKay, and Hughes. While the Harlem Renaissance did not achieve the sociopolitical transformation for which some had hoped, today it is clear that this movement marked a turning point in black cultural history both nationally and internationally: it helped to establish the authority of black writers and artists over the representation of black culture and experience, and it created for those writers and artists a continually expanding space within Western high culture.

TIMELINE

1905: The *Chicago Defender*, an African American newspaper, is founded in Chicago, Illinois.

1910: Crop damage sparks an economic depression in the South.

1910: The organization that would become the National Urban League is founded in New York City.

1915-1916: Blacks begin migrating in large numbers to cities in the North and West, in what would become known as the Great Migration.

1917: The United States enters World War I, and many blacks enlist to fight.

1917: A series of race riots, including the East Saint Louis Race Riot, break out around the country, reflecting white resentment of black workers in jobs previously held mainly by whites.

1917: Marcus Garvey establishes the Universal Negro Improvement Association in New York City.

1918: Harlem begins to draw black writers, artists, and intellectuals, becoming the cultural setting for the Harlem Renaissance.

1919: A series of about 25 violent race riots—resulting in the deaths of hundreds, mostly blacks—breaks out during what would become known as the Red Summer.

1925: Alain Locke publishes the widely influential work *The New Negro*, an anthology of works by black writers and a seminal text of the Harlem Renaissance.

1929: The Great Depression begins in the United States, causing widespread unemployment and worsening the economic situation of African Americans.

1933: In an effort to bring economic relief to the United States, President Franklin Delano Roosevelt launches the New Deal program, which helps bring economic reforms and opportunities to many, including African Americans.

MID-1930S: The Black Chicago Renaissance begins in the South Side of Chicago, centering in a neighborhood known as Bronzeville.

GLOSSARY

AESTHETIC A set of ideas or opinions about beauty or art.

AMELIORATIVE Of or relating to something that improves a condition or makes it less harmful.

ANTHOLOGY A collection of literary pieces.

ASSIMILATION The process whereby individuals or groups of differing ethnic heritage are absorbed into the dominant culture of a society. The process of assimilating involves taking on the traits of the dominant culture to such a degree that the assimilating group becomes socially indistinguishable from other members of the society.

BLACKFACE MINSTRELSY Indigenous American theatrical form that was performed by a group of white minstrels (traveling musicians) with black-painted faces, whose material caricatured the singing and dancing of slaves.

BLACK NATIONALISM U.S. political and social movement aimed at developing economic power and community and ethnic pride among African Americans.

CARICATURE Exaggeration of the actions, parts, or features of someone or something usually for comic or satirical effect.

CATALYST Someone or something that causes or speeds significant change or action.

CIVIL RIGHT Guarantees of equal opportunities and equal protection under the law, regardless of a person's sex, race, or religion.

DENIGRATION The act of making something seem less important or valuable.

DEPRESSION A period of low general economic activity with widespread unemployment.

FREE VERSE Poetry that does not rhyme and does not have a regular rhythm.

GHETTO A part of a city in which members of a particular group or race live, usually in poor conditions.

IDIOMATIC Peculiar to a particular group, individual, or style.

LURID   Causing horror or disgust; sensational.

MILITANT   Aggressively active (as in a cause); combative.

MISCEGENATION   Marriage or interbreeding between persons of different races.

PROPAGANDA   Ideas or statements that are often false or exaggerated and that are spread in order to help a cause, a political leader, a government, etc.

PROTAGONIST   The chief character in a play, novel, or story.

PUNDIT   A person who knows a lot about a particular subject and who expresses ideas and opinions about that subject publicly.

REVUE   A show in a theater that includes funny or satirical songs, dances, short plays, etc., usually about recent events.

SATIRE   Something meant to make fun of and show the weaknesses of human nature or a particular person.

SEGREGATION   The separation or isolation of a race, class, or group (as by restriction to an area or by separate schools).

SENSATIONALISM   The use of shocking details to cause a lot of excitement or interest.

SHARECROPPER   A farmer who works land for the owner in return for a share of the value of the crop.

SOCIAL REALISM   A style of art or literature that shows or describes social or political attitudes as they are in real life and rejects idealization.

SONNET   A poem made up of 14 lines that rhyme in a fixed pattern.

VAUDEVILLE   A type of entertainment that was popular in the United States in the late 19th and early 20th centuries and that had many different performers doing songs, dances, and comic acts.

VERNACULAR   The language of ordinary speech rather than formal writing.

FOR MORE INFORMATION

African American Museum in Philadelphia (AAMP)

701 Arch Street

Philadelphia, PA 19106

(215) 574-0380

Website: http://www.aampmuseum.org

The exhibits at the AAMP chronicle the political, social, cultural, and artistic history of African Americans from pre-colonial times to the present. Its collections and artifacts help preserve African American heritage and its traditions.

Association of African-Canadian Artists (AACA)

(416) 230-8615

Website: http://www.colour-blind.ca

The AACA supports and provides resources to African Canadian artists as part of its goal to promote African Canadian art. The AACA also sponsors an annual art exhibition that promotes art and awareness of issues in the African Canadian community.

The Givens Foundation for African American Literature

7151 York Avenue South

Minneapolis, MN 55435

(952) 831-2555

Website: http://www.givens.org

The Givens Foundation for African American Literature seeks to honor African American literature and authors and encourage future generations of writers. Through its various cultural outreach programs, the foundation brings prominent black writers to classrooms and supports local reading programs with a focus on black literature.

National Urban League

120 Wall Street

New York, NY 10005

(212) 558-5300

Website: http://nul.iamempowered.com

Founded during the Great Migration, the National Urban League
continues its long tradition of empowering underserved
communities. The organization supports initiatives in education,
employment, housing, and health care and advocates for civil
rights.

North American Black Historical Museum

277 King Street

Amherstburg, ON N9V 2C7

Canada

(519) 736-5433

Website: http://www.blackhistoricalmuseum.org

The artifacts preserved and presented by the North American
Black Historical Museum tell the story of African Canadians
through the centuries. Visitors can tour the museum's
collections or participate in one of its numerous events.

Schomburg Center for Research in Black Culture

515 Malcolm X Boulevard

New York, NY 10037

(917) 275-6975

Website: http://www.nypl.org/locations/schomburg

This research arm of the New York Public Library is committed to
researching, documenting, and preserving African American
history and culture. Visitors can explore its collections or
access its many resources for research purposes.

The Studio Museum in Harlem

144 West 125th Street

New York, NY 10027

(212) 864-4500

Website: http://www.studiomuseum.org

The Studio Museum in Harlem promotes the works of African
American artists and educates the public through lectures,
performances, and other programs. Its permanent collection
includes a number of works by Harlem Renaissance
photographer James VanDerZee.

Zora Neale Hurston National Museum of Fine Arts

227 E. Kennedy Boulevard

Eatonville, FL 32751

(407) 647-3307

Website: http://www.zoranealehurstonmuseum.com

The Hurston Museum showcases the works of African American
visual artists, including those influenced by Zora Neale
Hurston's literary works.

WEBSITES

Because of the changing nature of Internet links, Rosen Publishing has developed an online list of websites related to the subject
of this book. This site is updated regularly. Please use this link to
access this list:

http://www.rosenlinks.com/AAE/Migr

BIBLIOGRAPHY

Baldwin, Davarian L. *Chicago's New Negroes: Modernity, the Great Migration, and Black Urban Life*. Chapel Hill, NC: University of North Carolina Press, 2007.

Berlin, Ira. *The Making of African America: The Four Great Migrations*. New York, NY: Penguin, 2010.

Domina, Lynn. *The Harlem Renaissance: A Historical Exploration of Literature*. Santa Barbara, CA: Greenwood, 2015.

Harris, Leonard. *Alain L. Locke: The Biography of a Philosopher*. Chicago, IL: University of Chicago Press, 2008.

Johnson, Claudia Durst. *Race in the Poetry of Langston Hughes*. Detroit, MI: Greenhaven Press, 2014.

Jones, Ida E. *Mary McLeod Bethune in Washington, D.C.: Activism and Education in Logan Circle*. Charleston, SC: The History Press, 2013.

Kirschke, Amy Helene. *Women Artists of the Harlem Renaissance*. Jackson, MI: University Press of Mississippi, 2014.

Locke, Alain. *The New Negro: Voices of the Harlem Renaissance*. New York, NY: Touchstone, 1999.

Molesworth, Charles. *And Bid Him Sing: A Biography of Countee Cullen*. Chicago, IL: University of Chicago Press, 2012.

Plant, Deborah. *Zora Neale Hurston: A Biography of the Spirit*. Westport, CT: Praeger, 2011.

Reich, Steven A., ed. *The Great Black Migration: A Historical Encyclopedia of the American Mosaic*. Santa Barbara, CA: ABC-CLIO, 2014.

Wiener, Gary. *Women's Issues in Zora Neale Hurston's Their Eyes Were Watching God*. Detroit, MI: Greenhaven Press, 2012.

INDEX

A

Africa, 6, 23, 24, 31, 47
artists, 7, 25, 31, 45, 47, 49, 51,
    53, 67, 69, 70
arts, 5–6, 23, 25, 32, 45–55,
    56, 69

B

Baker, Josephine, 45, 55
Bethune, Mary McLeod, 59–60
black nationalism, 21, 23, 24, 25
Bontemps, Arna, 62, 64

C

Caribbean, 6, 25
Chicago, 8, 11–13, 18, 20, 59, 70
    renaissance in, 62, 64,
        66–67, 70
Chicago Defender, 11, 64, 70
civil rights, 6, 7, 16–17, 18,
    67, 68
civil rights movement, 6, 15
Cleveland, 11–13, 36
Columbia University, 14, 36, 40
Congress, 20, 68
Congress of Industrial
    Organizations (CIO), 62, 68
Crisis, The, 23, 31
crop damage, 4, 10, 70
Cullen, Countee, 29, 32, 36,
    47, 51

D

democracy, 15, 17
Detroit, 8, 11–13
discrimination, 14, 15, 23, 57,
    62, 69
Douglas, Aaron, 31, 45, 47, 49
drama, 42, 44, 66
Du Bois, W. E. B., 21, 23, 27

E

economic depression, 4,
    8–20, 70
economy, 23, 68
education, 4, 13, 14–15, 51, 59,
    60, 62
Elaine, Arkansas, 18, 20
equality, 10, 68, 69
Europe, 4, 15, 51, 53, 55

F

Fine Clothes to the Jew, 34, 36
Fisher, Rudolph, 32, 38
folklore, 40, 41, 44, 49

G

Garvey, Marcus, 21, 23, 24, 25,
    51, 70
ghettos, 4, 13, 24
Great Depression, 7, 34, 51,
    56–67, 68, 70